THE HOAX
OF HIGHER
CRITICISM

D1560296

Other books by Gary North

Marx's Religion of Revolution, 1968 [1988]
An Introduction to Christian Economics, 1973
Unconditional Surrender, 1981
Successful Investing in an Age of Envy, 1981
The Dominion Covenant: Genesis, 1982
Government By Emergency, 1983
The Last Train Out, 1983
Backward, Christian Soldiers?, 1984
*75 Bible Questions Your Instructors Pray
    You Won't Ask*, 1984
Coined Freedom: Gold in the Age of the Bureaucrats, 1984
*Moses and Pharaoh: Dominion Religion Versus
    Power Religion*, 1985
Negatrends, 1985
The Sinai Strategy, 1986
Conspiracy: A Biblical View, 1986
Unholy Spirits: Occultism and New Age Humanism, 1986
Honest Money, 1986
Fighting Chance, 1986 [with Arthur Robinson]
Dominion and Common Grace, 1987
Inherit the Earth, 1987
The Pirate Economy, 1987
Liberating Planet Earth, 1987
Healer of the Nations, 1987
Is the World Running Down?, 1988
Puritan Economic Experiments, 1988
Political Polytheism: The Myth of Pluralism, 1989
Tools of Dominion: The Case Laws of Exodus, 1989

Trespassing for Dear Life, 1989
When Justice Is Aborted, 1989
The Judeo-Christian Tradition, 1989
Pollution: A Biblical View, 1990
Slavery: A Biblical View, 1990
Victim Rights: A Biblical View, 1990

Books edited by Gary North

Foundations of Christian Scholarship, 1976
Tactics of Christian Resistance, 1983
The Theology of Christian Resistance, 1983
Editor, *Journal of Christian Reconstruction* (1974-1981)

THE HOAX OF HIGHER CRITICISM

Gary North

Institute for Christian Economics
Tyler, Texas

Published by the Institute for Christian Economics
Post Office Box 8000, Tyler, Texas 75711.

Typesetting by Nhung Pham Nguyen

Printed in the United States of America

ISBN 0-930464-30-3

TABLE OF CONTENTS

INTRODUCTION

I have given them thy word; and the world hath hated them, because they are not of the world, even as I am not of the world. I pray not that thou shouldest take them out of the world, but that thou shouldest keep them from the evil. They are not of the world, even as I am not of the world. Sanctify them through thy truth: thy word is truth (John 17:14-17).

Jesus' words were and are clear: without God's Word, His people cannot be sanctified — set apart from the world ethically, that is, clearly distinguished from this perishing world of sin. God sanctifies people by His Word. He makes *saints* of them. He gives them access to His *sanctuary* in prayer and worship. And He does this through His Word.

The Bible, all sixty-six books of the Old and New Testaments, is the revealed and written Word of God. It is the only visible manifestation of perfection in man's midst. It is the only unchangeable Word in history. It is the one and only completely reliable

1

source of ethics and law in history. It is the only written document which is on the one hand unchanging and in need of no revisions, yet which is also fully applicable to man and his environment throughout history. It is fixed, yet it applies to a world of historical change. It is, to use the language of philosophy, the "concrete universal."

Beware the Seducers

Most Christians have heard the New Testament verse, "All scripture is given by inspiration of God, and is profitable for doctrine, for reproof, for correction, for instruction in righteousness" (II Tim. 3:16). They may not remember the context of this verse, however. "But evil men and seducers shall wax worse and worse, deceiving, and being deceived. But continue thou in the things which thou hast learned and hast been assured of, knowing of whom thou hast learned them; And that from a child thou hast known the holy scriptures, which are able to make thee wise unto salvation through faith which is in Christ Jesus" (II Tim. 3:13-15).

Evil men continue to wax worse and worse over time, and they continue to deceive and be deceived. What is the antidote to their escalating evil? To continue steadfast in the things we have learned in the holy scriptures.

Evil men, not being stupid, have done whatever they could to discourage people's use of the holy scriptures. These strategies have included such things as 1) de-emphasizing the use of the Bible in worship and prayer and substituting church traditions and handbooks; 2) proclaiming newer revelations that supposedly are the updated Word of God; and 3) suppressing the production and sale of Bibles. Another effective strategy has been the development of a tradition of critical scholarship that seeks to prove that the Bible is not what it says it is, namely, the revealed Word of God. Instead, scholars present it as a disjointed collection of misleading documents, deliberately revised and rewritten by "redactors" and editors years or even centuries later than the texts initially appear to have been written. The Bible, in short, is a hoax.

Having made their case, they then adopt the language of praise, telling readers that, while mythical, the Bible is nevertheless a majestic document that deserves an important place in the varied and complex history of man's religions. In short, as hoaxes go, the Bible is a good one, as good or better than all the other hoaxes in man's religious history. This is the official "Party line" taken by every secular university in its comparative religion and "Bible as literature" courses, and also in most theological seminaries.

For over a century, such beliefs regarding the origin of the Bible have been common in academic circles. More important, the same beliefs have been increasingly prominent in evangelical Christian circles. And wherever such an attitude has taken root in evangelical churches, colleges, and seminaries, it has led, step by step, first to theological liberalism and then to political liberalism. Why? Because once the Bible is abandoned as the only source of unrevised and un-revisable stability in a world of ceaseless change, there is no other reliable rock for men to stand on. In the words of James, "he that wavereth is like a wave of the sea driven with the wind and tossed" (James 1:6). Men are tossed to and fro by the winds of opinion. In the twentieth century, the winds of opinion in the West have been liberal: inherently skeptical, doubt-filled, relativistic, and existentialist, challenged only by dogmatic Communism, which is now itself in the process of self-destructing ideologically and perhaps even institutionally.

Relativism cannot sustain a civilization, let alone reconstruct one. Thus, we are clearly at the end of an era, an era that began in the West over three centuries ago with the rise of Enlightenment skepticism. One of the marks of that self-conscious religious movement has been its commitment to the rejection of the Bible as the inspired and authoritative Word of God. Beginning in the late seventeenth century, Socinian-ism (a precursor of Unitarianism) and Deism steadily replaced Trinitarian Christianity in the thinking of the intellectual and political leaders of the West, be-ginning most importantly with Isaac Newton (who at least took seriously the Bible's historical texts),[1]

---

1. Isaac Newton, *The Chronology of the Ancient Kingdoms Amended*

and moving in ever-more openly heretical steps in the eighteenth century to Diderot, Rousseau, and Voltaire in Europe, as well as Hume and the Marquis de Sade, and in North America, to such figures as Franklin, John Adams, and Jefferson. (Jefferson actually produced his own highly expurgated Bible.)[2]

At this critical juncture in man's history, in a world now unified technologically and economically by the institutions of the West, the West is losing its nerve, just as Greece did over twenty centuries ago, and imperial Rome did seventeen centuries ago. The question today is: What will replace the Enlightenment-based West? A secondary question also needs to be dealt with: What will this transition cost?

The Illusion of Security

What we do know is that "you can't replace something with nothing." Thus, more than ever before in man's history, the whole world needs to be challenged by Elijah's question: "How long halt ye between two opinions? if the LORD be God, follow him: but if Baal, then follow him. And the people answered him not a word" (I Kings 18:21). The more things change, the more they stay the same. The silence of the people led

---

(1725). See Frank Manuel, *Isaac Newton Historian* (Cambridge, Massachusetts: Harvard University Press, 1963).

2. *The Life and Morals of Jesus of Nazareth Extracted textually from the Gospels.* Reprinted as *An American Christian Bible Extracted by Thomas Jefferson* (Rochester, Washington: Sovereign Press, 1982).

to the fire coming from heaven to destroy the sacrifice. Today, we face another kind of fire from the sky: man-made. We could become the sacrifice.

If Christians believe that they can escape their responsibility to publicly ask this question of ultimate sovereignty, and also escape the effects of the world's reply to this crucial question, they are living in a fantasy world. Many millions of fundamentalists have been living in just such a world.[3] But the world will not allow them to live in illusionary safety much longer.

If Christians lack confidence in the integrity and universal applicability of the Bible, Old and New Testaments, then they will not be able effectively to ask Elijah's public question. Men must be given an opportunity to decide self-consciously on their answer. There are now over five billion people alive today. Without saving faith in Jesus Christ, the vast majority of them will spend eternity in the lake of fire (Rev. 20:14). To save them, the Holy Spirit needs to make His move very soon. But if His own people continue to have doubts about God's Word, what will result from a worldwide revival? A much greater skepticism and a far greater sense of betrayal.

Thus, Christians need to regain their faith in God's Word. An important step in the recovery of such confidence is the acknowledgment, especially in the shat-

---

3. Dave Hunt, *Whatever Happened to Heaven?* (Eugene, Oregon: Harvest House, 1988).

tered seats of Christian learning, that higher criticism is a hoax.

1

THE ORIGIN OF
HIGHER CRITICISM

For had ye believed Moses, ye would have believed me, for he wrote of me. But if ye believe not his writings, how shall ye believe my words? (John 5:46-47).

So Jesus said to the Jewish leaders of His day in defense of His ministry and His person. They did not believe Him. Neither do their spiritual heirs today.

But it is not just Jews who refuse to take these words seriously; it is also the vast majority of those who graduate from theological seminaries today. With few exceptions, seminaries are staffed by professors of literature rather than professors of Christ. They have adopted a view of the Bible which says that the biblical texts reveal gross errors on the part of the Bible's writers and editors. The critics refer to the Bible as a myth-filled book. These classroom skeptics and their intellectual predecessors have labored for

9

over a century to remove Christians' confidence in
the accuracy of the Bible. Their personal goal, above
all other goals, is to escape the final judgment of the
God who has revealed Himself clearly. They comfort
themselves while discomforting their Bible-believing
students with this syllogism: "No permanent Bible,
no permanent law; no permanent law, no permanent
judgment." But this absence of God's judgment must
also be asserted with respect to history; higher criticism of the Bible plays a role in this dogma, too.

There is little doubt that the successful assault
on Christianity in the late-nineteenth century came
from two sources: Darwinism and higher criticism of
the Bible. The latter was exported primarily from German universities. The Christian West has been under
guerilla attack by German scholarship for about two
centuries. Prussians invented the government-sup-
ported kindergarten and the Ph.D. degree, two of the
most insidious inventions of the modern world. (I have
long appreciated the observation by literary critic
Edmund Wilson regarding the absurdity of the op-
pressive Ph.D. system. The world would be far better
off today "if, at the time of the First World War, when
we were renaming our hamburgers Salisbury Steak
and our sauerkraut Liberty Cabbage, we had decided
to scrap it as a German atrocity.")[1]

---

1. Edmund Wilson, *The Fruits of the MLA* (New York: New York
Review Book, 1968), p. 20. The MLA is the Modern Language As-
sociation.

Academic higher criticism of the Bible was nourished in its maturity in the same European corner of the academic world. It was promoted most successfully by intellectually disciplined German scholars in the nineteenth century. These men were dedicated to the destruction of orthodox Christianity. Their primary goal was to discover defects in the existing texts of Scripture, as well as to discover internal inconsistencies in the Bible's overall message. This strategy was designed to discredit the Christian world's faith in a permanent standard of righteousness. Higher criticism was the spiritual legacy of the Enlightenment, as one of its spiritual heirs frankly admits: "The rationalist Enlightenment radicalized the claim of reason and history; as a result it placed the claims of religion outside the realm of reason. In this division Orthodox theology lost its foundations in history. The cleft between reason and history triumphed among the learned — including theologians — and removed the basis of orthodoxy's epistemology."[2]

A War for English Civilization

What is not generally recognized, however, is that biblical higher criticism had its origin in the English-speaking world. It was English Deism rather than German scholarship that laid the intellectual founda-

---

2. Edgar Krentz, *The Historical-Critical Method* (Philadelphia: Fortress Press, [1975] 1977), p. 21.

tion of modern higher criticism. Even before Deism, certain aspects of the critical attack on the Bible, especially the Old Testament, had begun with Renaissance humanism.[3] R. K. Harrison traces back to mid-seventeenth-century rationalist political philosopher Thomas Hobbes the idea that the Pentateuch was compiled from much earlier sources written by Moses.[4]

Edgar Krentz is an enthusiastic defender of higher criticism against what he describes as the dogmatic church's "fear of change, fear of losing the basis for certainty of faith, and fear of posing questions in the area of authority."[5] He, too, identifies English Deism as the source of this intellectual development. "The eighteenth-century Deists treated the Bible with freedom when it did not, in their lights, accord with reason. For example, they argued that Isaiah was composite, the Gospels contradictory, and the apostles often unreliable."[6]

The Deists' attack on the divine authority of the Bible was not simply a product of the scholar's dusty study. It was closely associated with warring social and intellectual movements of the day. James Barr's

---

3. A little-known and unfortunately neglected study of the history of higher criticism is Henning Graf Reventlow, *The Authority of the Bible and the Rise of the Modern World* (Philadelphia: Fortress Press, [1980] 1984), Pt. I.

4. Roland Kenneth Harrison, *Introduction to the Old Testament* (Grand Rapids, Michigan: Eerdmans, [1969] 1974), pp. 9-10.

5. Krentz, *op. cit.*, p. 15.

6. *Ibid.*, p. 16.

observations are very important in understanding the roots of higher criticism and also in understanding the revival of biblical literalism as a social force in the United States, especially after 1960. The link between social action and biblical hermeneutics has been missed by most historians. Barr, following Reventlow's lead, does not make this mistake:

Church and state formed a single continuum, and political and theological questions were seen as interdependent. Questions about power and legitimacy rested in a high degree upon exegetical and interpretative ideas. In this the Old Testament — Reventlow's own specialism — was of primary importance. Even if the New Testament was the document of the earliest Christianity, the way in which the other collection of books form a yet older age, the Old Testament, was related to it. For it was the Old Testament, as it seemed, that offered guidance about king and state, about a commonwealth organized under divine statutes, about law and property, about war, about ritual and ceremony, about priesthood, continuity and succession. All of this was a disputed area from the Reformation onwards: because these were controversial matters in church and state, they generated deep differences in biblical interpretation. It was precisely because the Bible was assumed on all hands to be authoritative that it stimulated new notions about its own nature. It was because men sought answers to problems of life and society, as well as of thought and belief, that the Bible stimulated 'critical' modes of understanding itself.[7]

---

7. James Barr, "Foreword," Reventlow, *Authority of the Bible*, p. xiii.

Professor David Brion Davis' insights into the effects of Deism on Christian faith in Britain in the eighteenth and nineteenth centuries are also very important. He points out that the arguments of a handful of unpopular Deists in the early 1700's against the validity of the Old Testament called forth philosophical and theological defenses from orthodox Christians. But these defenses gave away too much to the haters of Christianity. Those Christians in our day who would disparage the laws of the Old Testament should take very seriously the implicit warning in Davis' observations:

By the 1730s Christian apologists had learned that disputes over textual details could never drain the deepening pools of doubt. As a compromise, it was sufficient to insist on the centrality of the resurrection and the historical fulfillment of Old Testament prophecy. As [Leslie] Stephen sums up the pragmatic resolution, Englishmen could still believe everything in the Bible, "but nothing too vigourously"; if the book was not flawless, it was "true enough for practical purposes."

So far as slavery is concerned, the Deists pointed toward the future position of [Thomas] Paine and Garrison. Thus God, by definition, was good and just. Yet the God of the Bible had authorized slavery as a divine punishment, along with such barbarities as the stoning to death of stubborn children who refused to obey their parents. It followed that the Bible could not be God's word.[8]

---

8. David Brion Davis, *The Problem of Slavery in the Age of Revolu-*

The heart of English Deism's attack on Christian orthodoxy was its faith in Newtonian natural law and hostility to Old Testament law and Old Testament prophecy. "If one could write off the Old Testament as testimony to a pre-Christian religion and vindicate the New Testament in another way (e.g. through its accord with the law of nature) Christianity could still be defended, albeit as a pedagogical means to the moral illumination of mankind."[9] Once the denial of the indissoluble unity of the Bible became common, the next step was easy: the denial of the need for an infallible New Testament in Christianity.

Reventlow has provided evidence of the political aspects of the war for and against the infallibility of the Bible. He provides over 400 pages of text and 200 pages of endnotes to demonstrate, among related themes, that "the political thought of the sixteenth, seventeenth and eighteenth centuries continually sought its models and arguments within the Bible, and the approach of each particular thinker in question provided the real criterion for the analogies drawn between the reconstructed biblical model and the principles which were normative for shaping the society of his time."[10] The Deists launched their war on the

---

tion, 1770-1823 (Ithaca, New York: Cornell University Press, 1975), p. 528.

9. Reventlow, *op. cit.*, p. 398.

10. *Ibid.*, p. 413.

Old Testament in an attempt to substitute natural law for biblical law. Anyone who fails to understand the ethical nature of this intellectual conflict does not understand the history of biblical higher criticism. The attack on the Old Testament was a fundamental aspect of the coming of modern humanist civilization.

Only as a result of the attack by Deists on the authority of Scripture (preparations for which were made, against their own intentions, by Latitudinarians, Locke and Newton), an attack which they made step by step, did the legacy of antiquity in the form of natural law and Stoic thought, which since the late Middle Ages had formed the common basis for thought despite all the changes of theological and philosophical direction, remain the one undisputed criterion. This produced a basically new stage both in the history of ideas and in the English constitution. This position already contains the roots of its own failure, in that the consistent development of the epistemological principles of Locke and Berkely [sic] by Hume soon showed that its basic presuppositions were untenable. However, two irreversible and definitive developments remained, which had made an appearance with it: the Bible lost its significance for philosophical thought and for the theoretical foundations of political ideals, and ethical rationalism (with a new foundation in Kant's critique) proved to be one of the forces shaping the modern period, which only now can really be said to have begun.[11]

Reventlow has pointed out that higher criticism

---

11. *Ibid.*, pp. 413-14.

has faded in importance since the end of the Second World War. In the immediate post-war era, biblical criticism was an important aspect of Protestant colleges and seminaries. No longer. "Given a predominant concern with the present and its seemingly urgent practical problems, which claim almost exclusive attention," he writes, "historical criticism and exegesis have come to take very much a back place."[12]

Burying the Dead

Why, then, should I devote a book to this topic? Because of a parallel process: while modern humanism has visibly begun to fragment, taking with it modern liberal theology, there has been a recovery of interest within the evangelical world of real-world questions that are best summarized under the general heading, "Christian worldview." The implicit dualisms of modern fundamentalism — Old Testament vs. New Testament, law vs. grace, letter vs. spirit, church vs. state, Israel vs. the church, eternity vs. history, heart vs. mind, dominion vs. rapture, culture vs. kingdom — have begun to be either discarded or at least seriously criticized from within the camp.[13] The Chris-

---

12. *Ibid.*, p. 1.

13. On the Israel-church dichotomy, see William E. Bell, A Critical Evaluation of the Pretribulation Rapture Doctrine in Christian Eschatology (Ph.D dissertation, New York University, 1968). See also John F. MacArthur, *The Gospel According to Jesus* (Grand Rapids, Michigan: Zondervan Academie, 1988). This book sold over 100,000

tian world's recovery of a vision of ethical unity, of a comprehensive world-and-life view, is basic to any workable strategy of Christian reconstruction. In this intellectual and emotional process of recovering Christianity's lost unity of vision, we are required to return to the original source of the problem: men's loss of faith in the unity of God's Word.

There is an old political slogan, "You can't beat something with nothing." Throughout the twentieth century, the Christian world has found itself in the position of battling something — self-confident humanism — with nothing: a philosophy of ethical dualism, a kind of Christian gnosticism.[14] This was obvious to everyone after the Scopes' "monkey" trial of 1925.[15] (In the early church, this dualistic philosophy which pitted the Old Testament against the New Testament was correctly identified by the church as heretical: Marcionism.) But the roles are now being reversed. Ever since the assassination of John F. Kennedy in November of 1963, Western humanism has steadily lost both its vision and its "can-do" confidence.[16] A

---

copies in hardback within a year of its publication. The survival of the older dualism is best represented by Dave Hunt, *Whatever Happened to Heaven?* (Eugene, Oregon: Harvest House, 1988).

14. Douglas W. Frank, *Less Than Conquerors: How Evangelicals Entered the Twentieth Century* (Grand Rapids, Michigan: Eerdmans, 1986).

15. George Marsden, *Fundamentalism and American Culture: The Shaping of Twentieth-Century Evangelicalism, 1870-1925* (New York: Oxford University Press, 1980), ch. 10: "The Great Reversal."

16. Gary North, *Unholy Spirits: Occultism and New Age Humanism*

similar loss of confidence also appeared in the mid-1980's behind the Iron and Bamboo Curtains. The implicit and inescapable dualism of all post-Kantian thought — fact vs. meaning, science vs. ethics, *phenomenal* vs. *noumenal*[17] — became a growing intellectual problem after the 1880's, and it could not, like Humpty Dumpty, be put back together again.[18] The social and political effects of this accelerating intellectual disorientation became clear to most social observers after 1963. Meanwhile, the appearance of Van Til's presuppositional apologetics in the mid-1940's,[19] the revival of biblical creationism after 1960,[20] and the preliminary recovery of the Puritan vision of the earthly victory of God's Kingdom have combined to produce a new intellectual perspective: Christian reconstruction.

Basic to this reversal has been the recovery of confidence by Christians in the reliability of the whole Bible. They have been presented with a growing body

(Ft. Worth, Texas: Dominion Press, 1986), Introduction.

17. Richard Kroner, *Kant's Weltanschauung* (Chicago: University of Chicago Press, [1914] 1956).

18. H. Stuart Hughes, *Consciousness and Society: The Reorientation of European Social Thought, 1890-1930* (New York: Knopf, 1958).

19. Cornelius Van Til, *The New Modernism: An Appraisal of the Theology of Barth and Brunner* (Philadelphia: Presbyterian & Reformed, 1946).

20. Henry M. Morris and John C. Whitcomb, Jr., *The Genesis Flood: The Biblical Record and Its Scientific Implications* (Philadelphia: Presbyterian & Reformed, 1961).

of evidence that Darwinism is a hoax. It is time for them to recognize that biblical higher criticism is an even older hoax, though related philosophically to Darwinism.

2

THE TECHNIQUES OF
HIGHER CRITICISM

*For we have not followed cunningly devised fables,
when we made known unto you the power and coming
of our Lord Jesus Christ, but were eyewitnesses of his
majesty (II Pet. 1:16).*

"Lower criticism" is the technical literary exercise of determining which of the existent ancient manuscripts of the Bible are authoritative and therefore belong in the canon of Scripture. Higher criticism, using similar techniques of analysis, and going mad in the process, argues that nothing in the canon of the Bible is what it appears to be, that the Creator God did not directly or uniquely inspire any of it, and that the scribes who assembled its component parts centuries after the fact were pathetic louts who were unable to follow the logic of any argument, or keep names straight for three consecutive pages, or even imitate the style of the previous lout who first made up some imaginary story and included it in an earlier manuscript. All of these "discoveries" are reached by means of supposedly precise literary techniques.

These textual critics regard the Bible as a kind of novel, so they apply to the study of the Bible techniques that are used in the literary criticism of fiction. Let me cite Wilson's comments on the absurdity of these techniques when applied to novels, let alone the Bible. He refers to an edition of Hawthorne's *Marble Faun*, edited by the University of Virginia's specialist in Elizabethan bibliography, Fredson Bowers. He does not spare Mr. Bowers.

But the fourth volume of the Centenary Edition of the works of Nathaniel Hawthorne, which contains only *The Marble Faun*, is the masterpiece of MLA bad bookmaking. I have weighed it, and it weighs nine pounds. It is 9 x 6$^1/_8$ inches, and 2$^3/_8$ inches thick. . . . *The Marble Faun*, since it is mainly Mr. Bowers's work, embodies the spirit of Mr. Bowers as no other of these volumes does. Of its 610 pages, the 467 of Hawthorne are weighed down by 89 pages of "Textual Introduction" and 143 pages of "Textual Notes." There are 44 pages of historical introduction preceding the textual introduction. We are told in these introductions, in accordance with the MLA formula, that, in the course of writing the book, the author, as novelists often do, changed the names of certain of the characters; and that many of the descriptions in it — as has been noted, also a common practice — have been taken from his Italian notebooks. This information is of no interest whatever. Nor is it of any interest to be told that Hawthorne's wife corrected certain inaccuracies in the Roman descriptions and otherwise made occasional suggestions, which Hawthorne did not always accept. It has evidently been trying for Mr. Bowers to find that, in the original manuscript, the author had been so inconsiderate as usually to make his changes "by wiping out with a finger while the ink was still wet and writing over the same space." But the places where these smudges occur have been carefully noted and listed. (It seems to me that this whole procedure meets an insurmountable obstacle when no corrected proofs survive that show the revisions of the author.)[1]

Wilson then asks the obvious question: "Now, what conceivable value have 276 pages of all this? Surely only that of gratifying the very small group of monomaniac bibliographers." He concludes, "The indiscriminate greed for this literary garbage on the part of universities is a sign of the academic pedantry on which American Lit. has been stranded."[2]

All of this is both accurate and amusing. But these same techniques of literary and textual criticism, when applied to biblical texts by monomaniacal German pedants and their epigone Anglo-American imitators, have for over a century undermined people's faith in the integrity of the Bible all over the world.[3]

---

1. Edmund Wilson, *The Fruits of the MLA* (New York: New York Review Book, 1968), pp. 18-19.

2. *Ibid.*, p. 20.

3. Krentz freely admits of literary criticism that "The four-

Apostate Deceivers

The higher critics present the Bible as a poorly assembled patchwork of lies and myths, and then they add insult to injury by arguing that their debunking operation somehow elevates our view of the Bible. For example, the internationally respected (unfortunately) Bible scholar G. Ernest Wright and his co-author argue that in the Bible, "What is important is what this great Lord has done."[4] But as soon as anyone raises the obvious question, "What exactly has God done?" the authors run for the cover of symbolism and supposed myth, in order to escape the Bible's detailed account of what God has done:

This furnishes a clue to our understanding of the prehistoric material preserved in Genesis 1-11. These traditions go far back into the dim and unrecoverable history of Israel; they are the popular traditions of a people, traditions which in part go back to a pre-Canaanite and North Mesopotamian background. For this reason there is little question of objective history here. We are instead faced

source theory of Pentateuchal origins and the two-source theory of the Synoptic interrelationships are its major results. Literary (source) criticism has achieved a more sharply contoured profile of the various sources and books, and the authors who stand behind them. It is indispensable for any responsible interpretation of the Bible." Edgar Krentz, *The Historical-Critical Method* (Philadelphia: Fortress Press, [1975] 1977), p. 50.

4. G. Ernest Wright and Reginald H. Fuller, *The Book of the Acts of God: Christian Scholarship Interprets the Bible* (Garden City, New York: Doubleday, 1957), p. 36.

with the question of why the old traditions were written down. What was the purpose of the writers who preserved them for us?[5]

Notice the shift in their argument. They tell us on the one hand that the Bible is a historical book, unique in the ancient world. The Bible's view of God rests squarely on what God has done in history. But when the key chapters that describe the creation of the universe and the Fall of man are brought up, as well as the Noachic flood and the tower of Babel, the authors immediately shift their focus away from what the Bible says about God; they shift their concern to what the Hebrews came later to *believe* about God. Their focus shifts from God to man. This is the essence of humanism. The fact is, their focus *began* with man rather than God — autonomous man.

The humanist scholar insists that we cannot deal with God, who is not an objective fact of history that can be studied. We can only deal with *men's recorded thoughts about God*, which are objective facts of history that can be studied. Van Til has summarized this humanistic impulse: "Men hope to find in a study of the *religious consciousness* something that has never been found before. They hope to find out what religion really is. The claim is made that now for the first time religion is really being studied from the inside."[6] Man's

5. *Ibid.*, p. 24.
6. Cornelius Van Til, *Psychology of Religion*, vol. IV of *In Defense*

religious consciousness becomes determinative in history, not the acts of God. Wright and Fuller should have titled their book, *The Book of the Surviving Early Writings of Two Religious Groups, Judaism and Christianity, Regarding the Acts of a God Who Does Not Really Interact With History*. Had they done so, of course, their academic charade would have been obvious from the beginning.

Historical Resurrection and Final Judgment

It is not only the creation of man and his subsequent fall from grace that must be discreetly covered up by the blanket of hypothetically objective history; it is also the resurrection of Christ. Both sin and redemption must be discussed apart from biblical revelation, for if the Bible's account of sin and redemption is taken seriously, then the issue of God's final judgment once again becomes a fundamental problem. This is the problem that autonomous man wishes most of all to avoid. So, the resurrection is relegated to the mythic past, and once again the authors focus on what a small group of people have thought about this non-historical event.

Finally, what shall we say about the resurrection of Christ, as understood in the New Testament? This cannot be an

of Biblical Christianity (Phillipsburg, New Jersey: Presbyterian & Reformed, 1971), p. 7.

objective fact of history in the same sense as was the crucifixion of Christ. The latter was a fact available to all men as a real happening, and pagan writers like Tacitus and Josephus can speak of it. But in the New Testament itself the Easter faith-event of the resurrection is perceived only by the people of the faith. Christ as risen was not seen by everyone, but only by the few. Easter was thus a reality for those in the inner circle of the disciples and apostles. That is not an arena where a historian can operate. Facts available to all men are the only data with which he can work, the facts available to the consciousness of a few are not objective history in the historian's sense.[7]

They distinguish the "real happening" of the crucifixion from the "faith-event" of the resurrection, which was an event of a very different character. Only "facts available to all men" — meaning facts that are implicitly possible for all men to have seen — are "real happenings." This means that the resurrection was somehow not a fact that in principle all men might have seen and verified, in the same way that they could have seen and verified the crucifixion. In other words, the resurrection was not a "real happening," although the calculating deceivers who wrote *The Book of the Acts of God* are too wise to say this blatantly, for fear of tipping their hand. They argue that the resurrection was therefore not an objective historical event, not "an objective fact of history."[8]

---

7. Wright and Fuller, *Acts of God*, p. 25.
8. On the anti-historical concept of the resurrection-event or faith-

The Bible tells a very different story. The fact of Christ's resurrection was sufficiently objective that Paul appealed to it as a commonly known fact when he defended himself in King Agrippa's court: "Why should it be thought a thing incredible with you, that God should raise the dead?" (Acts 26:8). He went on to remind skeptical Festus: "For the king knoweth of these things, before whom also I speak freely: for I am persuaded that none of these things are hidden from him; for this thing was not done in a corner" (Acts 26:26). And when Paul finished, Agrippa said to him: "Almost thou persuadest me to be a Christian" (Acts 26:28). But the higher critics are not even remotely persuaded. They see their man-appointed task to confuse Christians about the reliability of the orthodox faith, as well as to confuse non-Christians who might otherwise be persuaded.

A New Terminology

So, the critics have invented new terminology, the better to muddle the perceptions of their readers. For example, following the lead of Immanuel Kant's Protestant prophet Karl Barth, they substitute a grotesque hyphenated word like *faith-event* for the decisive and incriminating word, *fact*. "Hence we have to view the resurrection in the New Testament as a faith-event,

---

event in modern neo-orthodox theology, see Cornelius Van Til, *Christianity and Barthianism* (Philadelphia: Presbyterian & Reformed, 1962), pp. 92-113.

unlike other events, which is nevertheless real to the Christian community. It testifies to the knowledge that Christ is alive, not dead. The living Christ was known to be the head of the Church; and his power was real. The process, the how of Christ's transition from death to the living head of the new community, and the language used to describe that transition ('raised the third day,' 'Ascension,' 'going up,' 'sitting on the right hand of God') — these are products of the situation. They are the temporal language of the first-century Christians. To us, they are symbols of deep truth and nothing more, though they are symbols that are difficult to translate."[9]

Of course these are difficult symbols to translate, meaning *difficult to translate into historical categories that are acceptable to liberal humanism*, because "raised the third day" and "going up" meant exactly the same thing to a first-century Christian as they mean today. These hell-bound apostate scholars suffer from the problem Felix suffered when he heard the gospel from Paul, *fear*, for Felix trembled (Acts 24:25). They want to avoid thinking about the Bible's message of salvation, for it is also the message of God's inevitable final judgment. The biblical message of salvation is the only alternative to the biblical message of eternal torment.[10]

---

9. Wright and Fuller, *Acts of God*, p. 25.

10. Gary North, "Publisher's Epilogue," in David Chilton, *The Great Tribulation* (Ft. Worth, Texas: Dominion Press, 1987).

The higher critics have become the ultimate myth-makers by proclaiming the existence of a set of high ideals that are somehow associated with biblical myths (i.e., hoaxes). After telling the reader that the early chapters of Genesis are not historical, but simply symbolic, the authors assure us concerning the story of Adam's fall: "But let us not be deceived by the simple story form of presentation. The greatness of this story is its insight into the inner nature of man and the simple manner in which it presents that insight."[11] They first present evidence that, if true, any sensible reader — i.e., any non-Ph.D-holding higher critic — would recognize clearly as evidence that the Bible is a gigantic hoax, and then they speak as though this "new, improved" understanding of the Bible will lead society to higher ideals and moral righteousness. They are classic examples of C. S. Lewis' description of modern humanist culture: "In a sort of ghastly simplicity we remove the organ and demand the function. We make men without chests and expect of them virtue and enterprise. We laugh at honour and are shocked to find traitors in our midst. We castrate and bid the geldings be fruitful."[12]

What the higher critics want us to believe in is the world according to Immanuel Kant, a dialectical realm composed of two utterly separate worlds: the

---

11. Wright and Fuller, *Acts of God*, p. 61.

12. C. S. Lewis, *The Abolition of Man* (New York: Macmillan, [1947] 1965), p. 35.

phenomenal world of historical facts — meaningless historical facts apart from man's interpretations of them — and the trans-historical noumenal world of human meaning — utterly timeless, non-cognitive meaning — that is completely distinct from the phenomenal world of measurable cause and effect.[13] Autonomous man stands at the intersection of these two dialectical realms, and somehow creates meaning for himself. God is given homage only as the unknown god of the Greeks (Acts 17:23), and even worse, as the inherently *unknowable* god. An unknowable god is the only god who is acceptable to modern autonomous man, for an unknowable god presumably will not bring final judgment to inherently uninformed and uninformable finite mankind. We must never forget: *the primary goal of self-proclaimed autonomous man is to escape God's final judgment.* So, in order to escape this judgment, the higher critics spin a web of pompous verbiage that they hope and pray — well, at least they hope — will protect them from the eternal consequences of their God-defying rebellion.

Who Is the Hoaxer?

Our authors ask three rhetorical questions, and then give their hapless readers a bowl of lukewarm mental mush in reply. First, the questions: "Yet there

---

13. Richard Kroner, *Kant's Weltanschauung* (Chicago: University of Chicago Press, [1914] 1956).

is always the final lurking question: Is the Bible true? What is truth and what is just symbolic? Cannot I have anything that is absolutely certain?" Then the mush: "The answer must be that the symbol *is* the truth. We have no other truth. We know it is not literal truth, but we know that the biblical portrayal is the relationship between the unknown infinite and ourselves here and now. No precise dividing line can be drawn between the ultimately real and the poetic symbol, because God has not made us infinite."[14] In short, they argue that because I am not infinite, and therefore not God, I need not fear an infinite God, for my very finitude keeps me from knowing God. To which Paul answered many centuries ago:

For the wrath of God is revealed from heaven against all ungodliness and unrighteousness of men, who hold [back] the truth in unrighteousness; because that which may be known of God is manifest in them; for God hath shewed it unto them. For the invisible things of him from the creation of the world are clearly seen, being understood by the things that are made, even his eternal power and Godhead; so that they are without excuse (Rom. 1:18-20).

The Bible of the higher critics cannot possibly be what it says clearly that it is: the revealed Word of the Creator and Judge of the universe. Now, if the Bible really isn't what it says it is, then it must be a hoax. Once the implicit though politely unstated accusa-

---

14. Wright and Fuller, *Acts of God*, p. 37.

tion of hoaxing is made, the question then arises: Who is the true hoaxer, God or the higher critic? There should be no doubt in our minds: the literary critic is the myth-maker. Literary higher criticism of the Bible is a hoax. No other word does it justice. It is a fraud, a lie, a denial that God's revealed Word is what it says it is.[15] Wright and Fuller made a classic Freudian slip when they used the word *forged* for "hammered out" (as in "crucible"), when it is far easier to interpret *forged* as "falsified" (as in "forged signature"): "It is quite legitimate to use the methods of historical and literary criticism which were forged during the liberal period in order to reconstruct the underlying history."[16] Forged indeed! Higher criticism rests on the presupposition that all morality is relative to historical time and place, and that the laws of the Bible, a strictly historical human document, are also relative. It denies the unity and moral integrity of the Bible.

---

15. Oswald T. Allis, *The Five Books of Moses* (Philadelphia: Presbyterian & Reformed, [1943] 1949). I appreciate the book's subtitle, reminiscent of the nineteenth century: *A Reexamination of the Modern Theory that the Pentateuch Is a Late Compilation from Diverse and Conflicting Sources by Authors and Editors Whose Identity Is Completely Unknown.* See also Allis, *The Old Testament: Its Claims and Its Critics* (Nutley, New Jersey: Presbyterian & Reformed, 1972); Robert Dick Wilson, *A Scientific Investigation of the Old Testament*, with revisions by Edward J. Young (Chicago, Illinois: Moody Press, 1959); Edward J. Young, *Thy Word Is Truth* (Grand Rapids, Michigan: Eerdmans, 1957).

16. Wright and Fuller, *Acts of God*, p. 237.

Criticizing Textual Criticism

The methods used by higher critics are circular: they use their colleagues' reconstructed literary texts to reconstruct the biblical past, and they use their own newly reconstructed biblical past to further reconstruct the biblical texts. On and on the academic game goes, signifying nothing except the futile purposes to which very dull people's minds can be put.

These literary techniques are highly complex, yet amazingly shoddy. The practitioners agree on very little; they reach no testable conclusions; and their required techniques absorb inordinate quantities of time to master. Liberal Bible scholar Calum Carmichael puts it mildly when he warns his readers: "Historical and literary criticism is undeniably useful when working with ancient sources, but not only has it limitations, it sometimes leads nowhere. One manifest restriction in its application to most biblical material is that the historical results hypothesized cannot be corroborated. The speculative character of most such results is easily overlooked because the historical method is so deeply entrenched in scholarly approaches. With a little distance, we can see just how shaky the historical method is. . . . The procedure is a dispiriting one, dull to read, difficult to follow, and largely illusory given the paucity of the results and the conjectured historical realities dotted here and there over a vast span of time. Its most depressing aspect is the no doubt unintentional demeaning of the intelligence of the lawgiver who was responsible for the presentation of the material available to us. E. M. Forster, struck by the cavalier way in which we treat the past, attributed the attitude to the fact that those who lived then are all dead and cannot rise up and protest."[17]

He is being much too kind. The scholars' "demeaning of the intelligence of the lawgiver who was responsible for the presentation of the material available to us" is all too intentional, for that Lawgiver is God Almighty, who will judge every man on judgment day. Higher critics are determined to deny that such a cosmic Lawgiver exists, and they do their best to make His laws seem like an incoherent collection of disjointed and self-contradictory pronouncements, a judicial jumble compiled by a series of editors who apparently could not keep clear in their minds anything that was written in the text in front of them that was farther back or farther forward than three lines. Somehow, these deceptive ancient masters of language and textual subtleties could not keep any argument straight, or remember the plot line of even a one-page story. Their heavy-handed attempts to revise the ancient texts for their own contemporary purposes were so badly bungled that they succeeded only in so dis-

---

17. Calum M. Carmichael, *Law and Narrative in the Bible: The Evidence of the Deuteronomic Laws and the Decalogue* (Ithaca, New York: Cornell University Press, 1985), p. 14.

torting the text that no careful reader could possibly believe that God had revealed the Pentateuch to one man, Moses.

It is not the Pentateuch that is disjointed. It was not the hypothetical "later editors" who could not keep things straight in their minds. Rather, it is the paid professional army of higher critics. I appreciate C. S. Lewis' comments, as a master of medieval and early modern English literature, regarding the ability of textual critics to understand their texts: "These men ask me to believe they can read between the lines of old texts; the evidence is their obvious inability to read (in any sense worth discussing) the lines themselves. They claim to see fern-seed and can't see an elephant ten yards away in broad daylight."[18]

---

18. C. S. Lewis, *Christian Reflections*, edited by Walter Hooper (London: Geoffrey Bles, 1967), p. 157. The essay is titled, "Modern Thought and Biblical Criticism."

3

THE ETHICS OF
HIGHER CRITICISM

*For men shall be lovers of their own selves, covet-
ous, boasters, proud, blasphemers, disobedient to parents, unthankful, unholy, without natural affection, truce-
breakers, false accusers, incontinent, fierce, despisers of
those that are good, traitors, heady, highminded, lovers
of pleasures more than lovers of God; having a form of
godliness, but denying the power thereof: from such turn
away. For of this sort are they which creep into houses,
and lead captive silly women laden with sins, led away
with divers lusts, ever learning, and never able to come
to the knowledge of the truth (II Tim. 3:2-7).*

The real motive of higher criticism is ethical. This,
too, has been Van Til's assertion: covenant-breaking
man's problem is not a lack of knowledge about God;
rather, it is his *lack of obedience* to God. The higher
critics seek to confuse men by blurring the universal

ethical requirements of God's holy Word. If they were correct, then there could be no final judgment, for God's sanctions require God's permanent stipulations. To deny God's judgment, His stipulations must be presumed to be incoherent, unclear, and limited to the individual conscience, rather than coherent, clear, and universal in every human conscience.

Karl Barth was a defender of just such a radically individual ethics, an ethics which matched his thesis of a radically dialectical, incoherent, creed-denying, God-man encounter — a noumenal encounter beyond nature and history. He denied as "untenable" the assumption of the universality of God's ethical commands, for "the command of God . . . is always an individual command for the conduct of this man, at this moment and in this situation. . . ."[1] In short, on Barth's basis there cannot be a God-revealed permanent Christian ethics, nor civil statutes that conform to fixed biblical principles. Statutes and creeds are supposedly only the inventions of men, not the appropriate human responses to God's fixed and reliable revelation of Himself in a God-inspired historical document. Barth thereby proclaimed the triumph of Kant's noumenal trans-historical realm of randomness over Kant's phenomenal historical realm of sci-

---

1. Karl Barth, *Church Dogmatics*, translated by A. T. Mackay (Edinburgh: T. & T. Clark, 1961), Vol. 3, Part 4, p. 11; cited by Walter Kaiser, Jr., *Toward Old Testament Ethics* (Grand Rapids, Michigan: Zondervan Academie, 1983), p. 25.

entifically predictable cause and effect, all in the name
of a higher ethics and higher critical insights. This
was Barth's assertion of the triumph of historical and
ethical relativism over the Bible. This was his an-
nouncement of the triumph of covenant-breaking man
over God, and above all, over the final judgment.
Autonomous man seeks to impose his temporal judg-
ments on God by denying the historic validity of God's
revelation of Himself. This, of course, was precisely
what Adam attempted to do in the garden by eating
the forbidden fruit in defiance of God's explicit revelation. The results are equally predictable.

Permanent Standards for Eternal Judgment

A righteous God who judges men eternally does
so only on the basis of a *unified ethical system*. Only
because the ethical standards never change could the
punishment never change. If the texts are not ethically unified, then there is no threat to man from the
God of the Bible. Thus, the "prime directive" of higher
criticism is to affirm the lack of unity in the Bible.
This is the "higher" critic's operating presupposition
when he begins to study the Bible.

He adopts a five-step process. First, he *assumes*
that the books of the Bible are textually jumbled. Second, he tries to *prove* that the books of the Bible are
textually jumbled. Third, he *assumes* that through crea-
tive myth-making, he himself can produce a mean-

ingful reconstruction of what the ancient authors ("redactors") really wanted to convey to all mankind, despite each one's short-term goals of political or bureaucratic manipulation. Fourth, he tries to present a *"deeper" message* for modern man that transcends the Bible's unfortunately jumbled texts. Finally, the higher critic offers *his version of the Bible's true transcendent ethical unity.* Somehow, this newly discovered transcendent ethical unity always winds up sounding like the last decade's political manifesto for social democracy, or else it sounds like Marxism.

A good statement of this operating presupposition of textual disunity is J. L. Houlden's remark that "There is, strictly speaking, no such thing as 'the X of the New Testament'. . . . It is only at the cost of ignoring the individuality of each, in thought and expression, that the unified account can emerge. . . . There can be no initial assumption of harmony."[2] So, it is supposedly illegitimate to speak of "the X of the New Testament." Well, how about a *heavenly Author* of the New Testament? How about solving the equation as "X = God." Sorry, says Houlden implicitly, we cannot begin with any such assumption. Well, then, how about "the *grammar* of the New Testament"? We will posit "X = grammar." Houlden is then silent, as befits a man who has implicitly denied the grammati-

---

2. J. L. Houlden, *Ethics and the New Testament* (Middlesex, England: Penguin, 1973), p. 2; cited by Kaiser, *ibid.*, p. 13.

cal coherence of New Testament Greek. If he follows the logic of his statement, Greek grammar disappears, and with it, grammar in general. The coherence of the universe of rational discourse disappears, not to mention coherence of the universe itself. Once you play these sorts of verbal games, their self-contradictory nature swallows up your vaunted neutral scholarship.

Contrary to Mr. Houlden, we must begin our Bible studies (and every other kind of study) with the presupposition of the self-contained ontological Trinity and His creation of the universe out of nothing. We must begin with the Creator-creature distinction, as Van Til affirmed throughout his career. We must begin with the assumption of the unity and harmony of God's expression of Himself in the Word of God, the Bible. If we do not begin with this set of presuppositions, we will find ourselves as intellectually impotent as the scholarly higher critics of the Bible, who find it difficult to make sense of anything.

The Party Line

The higher critics are always alert to any hint of defection from the Party line concerning ethical relativism. Hans Jochen Boecker criticizes the Postscript of another German scholar, H. -D. Bracker. Herr Doctor Bracker made an academic gaffe by concluding in 1962 that "Israel's law by far surpassed the other three [Babylonian, Hittite and Assyrian] in its ethical

purity and in its humanity." Such a conclusion is
"highly suspect," Herr Doctor Boecker assures his readers.[3] Why is this conclusion "highly suspect"? Because
it breaks with the supposed academic neutrality and
ethical relativism of modern scholarship, especially
modern biblical scholarship.

Young scholars are informed subtly from the out-
set of their careers as undergraduates that they must
always begin with the assumption that all religious
faiths are equal (except for fundamentalism, which
preaches an infallible Bible), all political systems are
equal (except for Nazi Germany's, of course, mainly
because the Nazis lost the war, and South Africa's,
which is not based on the politics of black Africa: "one
man, one vote, one time only"), and all nations are
equal (except for the United States, which occasion-
ally dares to call the Soviet Union into question). What
this kind of worldview produces is men without spines
who cannot distinguish truth from falsehood, righteousness from perversion, or a cause worth dying for
from the latest political slogan. It is only by the common grace of God that they can distinguish AIDS
from scarlet fever, except that they probably think
that people with scarlet fever should be quarantined.

So, in order to prove all this, higher critics self-

---

3. Hans Jochen Boecker, *Law and the Administration of Justice in the
Old Testament and Ancient East*, translated by Jeremy Moiser (Minnea-
polis, Minnesota: Augsburg, [1976] 1980), p. 16.

consciously spend their myopia-inducing lives search-
ing for internal evidence that denies the unity of that
historical document. I agree with Walter Kaiser's observation of the crucial link between higher criticism
and men's loss of faith in the unity of the biblical
message (including its ethical requirements): "For
many it is too much to assume that there is consis-
tency within one book or even a series of books al-
leged to have been written by the same author, for
many contend that various forms of literary criticism
have suggested composite documents often tradition-
ally posing under one single author. This argument,
more than any other argument in the last two hun-
dred years, has been responsible for cutting the main
nerve of the case for the unity and authority of the
biblical message."[4]

Higher Criticism and Evolution

Higher criticism is based on an evolutionary model
of human morality and human history. It assumes,
and then seeks to prove, that the texts of the Bible,
and especially the Old Testament, were self-consciously altered by later scribes and "redactors" in
order to make the Bible's message conform to the latest ethical and economic principles of the day. It
helped to create the early nineteenth century's intellectual climate of opinion that was so favorable to

---

4. Kaiser, *Toward Old Testament Ethics*, p. 26.

Darwinism after 1859. Ethical relativism is an idea that has had pernicious consequences. Someday, some enterprising scholar is going to write a monograph tracing at least one of the historic roots of Nazism back to German higher criticism. Nazism has been traced back to just about everything else in German history, but this possibility has been regarded as off-limits by secular historians; it comes too close to home, theologically speaking. D. F. Strauss' *Life of Jesus* could easily serve as a starting point in such an investigation. Arthur Cohen has suggested this historical connection, and it deserves a detailed study.[5] Cohen's warning should be taken seriously: it is dangerous to separate ethics from faith, which is what higher criticism did. "Nineteenth-century theologians had, indeed, succeeded: the ethics of the Hebrew Bible were winnowed by the Gospels and the ethics restored to Christian conscience were ethics for the 'between time,' when history awaited the return of Christ. The purge of Christianity of its Jewish elements was disastrous."[6]

A representative academic example of the spoiled fruits of higher criticism is presented by the economic historian Morris Silver, who spends an entire volume painstakingly trying to collate and make coherent an immense body of archeological, economic, and higher

---

5. Arthur A. Cohen, *The Myth of the Judeo-Christian Tradition* (New York: Schocken, 1971), pp. 199-200.

6. *Ibid.*, p. 200.

critical textual evidence in order to prove what higher critics assume, namely, that the Book of Deuteronomy was written many centuries after the exodus. "A central hypothesis of this book is that Deuteronomy represents an attempt to revise and expand the old divine-law code *and thereby the legal practices of the Israelite state* in the light of the circumstances of a much more affluent society."[7] That his presentation of the evidence is painful to follow, let alone remember, should come as no surprise: he combines a false initial hypothesis with hundreds of disjointed citations from far too disjointed a body of scholarship.

There is another major intellectual goal of higher criticism besides re-dating the giving of God's laws in order to relativize them: re-dating every document in which a specific prophecy later came true. The author of the prophecy must have written it after the prophesied event took place. Thus, the so-called prophecy is regarded as merely a convenient lie on the part of a redactor, i.e., a myth. Even when this tactic of re-dating is not invoked, higher critics remain skeptical of all future-predicting prophecies. Jeremiah prophesied the death of the false prophet Hananiah, and Hananiah died later that year (Jer. 28:15-17). Silver asks rhetorically: "Does this story represent myth, hypnotic suggestion, coincidence, or political assassina-

---

7. Morris Silver, *Prophets and Markets: The Political Economy of Ancient Israel* (Boston: Kluwer-Nijhoff, 1983), p. 230.

tion?"[8] What it could not possibly represent, in his worldview, is a fulfilled prophecy.

If a person derives ethics from history, and then scrambles the historical data by means of an erroneous chronological scheme, both his ethics and his historiography will flounder.[9] He will write such nonsense as this: ". . . the indispensable agricultural-fertility aspect of Baalism[10] had long ago become a traditional part of Yahweh worship, taken for granted even by Amos and Hosea. It is a naive misconception to suppose that the latter had achieved its final form even at the time of Moses and the Exodus. As Morgenstern[11] well notes, the Jewish religion is the product of historical evolution to meet the needs of the Jewish people 'from the remote desert period to the present

---

8. *Ibid.*, p. 140.

9. There are few intellectual tasks more pressing on Christian historians of the ancient Near East and classical Greece and Rome than to rethink the various chronologies prior to about 750 B.C. Cf. Gary North, *Moses and Pharaoh: Dominion Religion vs. Power Religion* (Tyler, Texas: Institute for Christian Economics, 1985), Appendix A: "The Reconstruction of Egypt's Chronology."

10. Citing Ivan Engnell, *Studies in Divine Kingship in the Near East* (Oxford: Basil Blackwell, [1943] 1967), p. 172.

11. Julian Morgenstern, *Rites of Birth, Marriage, Death and Kindred Occasions Among the Semites* (Cincinnati, Ohio: Hebrew Union College Press, 1966), p. 64. If any single individual was most responsible for corrupting American Judaism by means of higher criticism, it was the remarkable, long-lived Julian Morgenstern. For a summary of his life, see Morris Lieberman, "Julian Morgenstern — Scholar, Teacher and Leader," *Hebrew Union College Annual*, XXXII (1961), pp. 1-9.

day.' The only 'pure Yahwism' is a dead Yahwism."[12] The book's bibliography is impressive, but its conclusions are trivial on those occasions when they are correct. Such is the endlessly repeated fate of two centuries of higher critical scholarship and historical studies based on higher criticism: the academic trumpets sound, and a mouse marches out, dragging behind him a mountain of jumbled chronologies and footnotes to obscure, unread, and unreadable journal articles, leaving behind him a trail of droppings for other busy mice to follow.

Higher criticism is today a backwater academic discipline that serves the needs of humanism by keeping linguistically skilled but stylistically handicapped scholars fully employed. It also serves to keep educated Christians confused about the legitimacy of their God-given marching orders. Christian scholars pay a great deal of attention to the latest findings of higher critics, filling their own unread academic journals with vaguely conservative modifications of, and an occasional refutation of, some unread essay in a higher critical academic journal. In contrast, secular scholars today pay very little attention to higher criticism's methods or its findings. This speaks far better of secular scholars than for neo-evangelical scholars who have succumbed to the siren song of certified academic respectability, and who have adopted an attitude of "me,

---

12. Silver, *Prophets and Markets*, p. 124.

too, but not quite so radical, at least not yet."

I do not deny that an occasional linguistically gifted scholar such as Robert Dick Wilson, O. T. Allis, or Edward J. Young should devote a lifetime to refuting the best and most influential of the higher critics' presentations. This is a subdivision of apologetics — the intellectual defense of the faith. But surely there is little need for Christians to subsidize the bulk of what passes for academic Old Testament studies today: narrowly focused essays that prove or disprove theses that no one considers relevant, theses that will almost surely be abandoned in less than five years, in those rare instances that anyone adopts them in the first place.

CONCLUSION

Jesus said unto him, Let the dead bury their dead:
but go thou and preach the kingdom of God (Luke 9:60).

Christians have made the mistake of regarding the debates over higher criticism as being the peculiar habit of linguistic specialists and theologians. The fact is, from the very beginning of the rise of humanism, there has been a war between those who defend the Bible, especially the Old Testament, and those who reject this testimony. This debate throughout most of its history involved all of culture, what we call today a conflict between comprehensive world-and-life views. It is only in the hands of modern scholars that the debate has been narrowly focused on the technical issues of textual analysis. Earlier generations recognized that the debate was far more important than modern scholars are willing to admit.

The task of the Christian scholar in defending the Bible as the Word of God must not be narrowly focused. The debate did not originate in the university library; it originated in the social conflicts of the day. The participants understood that the outcome of this academic debate over the textual integrity of the Bible would determine who would gain and retain control of the seats of power. This conflict was a life-and-death matter for English culture in the early modern period, and it was recognized as such by the participants.

This perception of the magnitude of the debate has been lost on modern Bible scholars. Humanists have rewritten history in order to downplay the importance of the Bible in Western thought and culture. Evangelical Christians have generally agreed to this view of Western history, almost by default. Members of the evangelical scholarly world have been trained by the humanists who control access to the major institutions of higher learning (i.e., trade union certification). At the same time, laymen in the pews have also accepted the humanists' view of the peripheral nature of the Bible's influence in the early modern history because such a view of the Bible's lack of relevance in history conforms to the mind-set of what has been called the left wing of the Reformation: Anabaptist pietism. This tradition has been at war with Old Testament law from the beginning. Indeed, this movement was one of the forerunners of higher criticism, for it contrasted the Bible with the inner testimony of man's spirit, and elevated the latter over the former.[1]

---

1. Henning Graf Reventlow, *The Authority of the Bible and the Rise*

This legacy of the internalization of the Word of God triumphed in the modern church through the influence of twentieth-century fundamentalism: grace over law.[2] Once again, we see evidence of the implicit alliance between the power religion and the escape religion.

It is time for Christian scholars of the Old Testament to stop their fruitless shadow-boxing with higher critics who will no more listen to Bible-defending scholars than they have listened to Moses and Christ. It is time for orthodox Bible scholars to go to the Pentateuch to find out what it says, not to discover some new bit of evidence that Moses really and truly did say it. There is no doubt a place in the division of intellectual labor for linguistically skilled Christians to defend the integrity of the Bible against the incoherent slanders of higher critics, but this technical task should be put on a low-priority basis. What we do need is a great deal of research on the chronology of the Pentateuch — not on when Moses wrote the Pentateuch, but on what was going on in the surrounding nations at the time of the exodus. We need a reconstruction of ancient chronology, one based on the presupposition that the Bible gives us the authoritative primary source documents, not Egypt or Babylon. Such a project would keep a lot of linguistically

---

of the Modern World (Philadelphia: Fortress Press, [1980] 1985), ch. 3.

2. Douglas W. Frank, *Less Than Conquerors: How Evangelicals Entered the Twentieth Century* (Grand Rapids, Michigan: Eerdmans, 1986).

skilled scholars productively busy for several generations.

Meanwhile, let the higher critics drown in their own footnotes, the way that Arias died by falling head-first into a privy.[3] Let the dead bury the dead, preferably face down in a scholarly journal.

---

3. R. J. Rushdoony, *Foundations of Social Order: Studies in the Creeds and Councils of the Early Church* (Fairfax, Virginia: Thoburn Press, [1969] 1978), p. 17.

BIBLIOGRAPHY

The following books represent an introduction to the topic of the higher criticism of the Bible. The first section lists books in English by defenders of the infallibility of Scripture. The second section lists materials dealing with the long-neglected and crucial topic of ancient chronology.

It is my contention that the single greatest failure of modern anti-critical Bible scholars is their acceptance of the humanists' timetables, especially prior to 750 B.C. The humanists have for over a century rested a significant part of their case against the Old Testament on their own reconstruction of the chronology of Egypt, which they accept as definitive, despite the fact that the Egyptians cared little for chronology and time-based historical records. This ready acceptance of humanist timetables has led Christian scholars time and again into pitfalls, especially their attempts to identify certain mummified pharaohs as the pharaoh of the exodus. It has also led

Bible-affirming scholars to an acceptance of a late date for the exodus (post-1445 B.C.), a compromise which is the equivalent of a slippery slide toward a cliff.

Textual Criticism

Allis, Oswald T. *The Five Books of Moses*. Second edition, 1949. Phillipsburg, New Jersey: Presbyterian & Reformed.

——————— . *The Old Testament: Its Claims and Its Critics*. 1972. Nutley, New Jersey: Presbyterian & Reformed.

Archer, Gleason. *A Survey of Old Testament Introduction*. 1964. Chicago: Moody Press.

Guthrie, Donald. *New Testament Introduction*. 1971. Downers Grove, Illinois: InterVarsity Press.

Harris, R. Laird. *Inspiration and Canonicity of the Bible*. 1957. Grand Rapids, Michigan: Zondervan.

Harrison, Roland K. *Introduction to the Old Testament*. Second edition, 1974. Grand Rapids, Michigan: Eerdmans.

Reventlow, Henning Graf. *The Authority of the Bible and the Rise of the Modern World*. (1980) 1984. Philadelphia: Fortress Press.

Wilson, Robert Dick. *A Scientific Investigation of the Old Testament*. Revisions by Edward J. Young. 1959 edition. Chicago: Moody Press.

Young, Edward J. *An Introduction to the Old Testament*.

Revised edition, 1960. Grand Rapids, Michigan: Eerdmans.

————————— . *Thy Word Is Truth*. 1949. Grand Rapids, Michigan: Eerdmans.

Chronological Reconstruction

Courville, Donovan. *The Exodus Problem and Its Ramifications*. 1971. Loma Linda, California: Challenge Books.

Fell, Barry. *Bronze Age America*. 1982. Boston: Little, Brown.

————————— . *Saga America*. 1980. New York: Times Books.

Gentry, Kenneth. *The Beast of Revelation*. 1989. Tyler, Texas: Institute for Christian Economics.

————————— . *Before Jerusalem Fell: Dating the Book of Revelation*. 1989. Tyler, Texas: Institute for Christian Economics.

de Grazia, Alfred, editor. *The Velikovsky Affair: The Warfare of Science and Scientism*. 1966. New Hyde Park, New York: University Books.

Newton, Isaac. *The Chronology of the Ancient Kingdoms Amended*. 1725.

North, Gary. *Moses and Pharaoh: Dominion Religion vs. Power Religion*. 1985. Tyler, Texas: Institute for Christian Economics. Appendix A: "The Reconstruction of Egypt's Chronology."

Taylor, Charles. *Rewriting Bible History (According to Scripture)*. 1984. 84 Northgate Street, Unley Park, South Australia: House of Tabor.

Thiele, Edwin R. *A Chronology of the Hebrew Kings*. 1977. Grand Rapids, Michigan: Zondervan.

_____ . *The Mysterious Numbers of the Hebrew Kings*. New edition, 1984. Grand Rapids, Michigan: Zondervan.

Velikovsky, Immanuel. *Ages in Chaos*. 1952. Garden City, New York: Doubleday.

_____ . *Oedipus and Akhnaton*. 1960. Garden City, New York: Doubleday, 1960.

_____ . *Peoples of the Sea*. 1977. Garden City, New York: Doubleday.

_____ . *Ramses II and His Time*. 1978. Garden City, New York: Doubleday.

Scholarly Journals:
Epigraphic Society Occasional Publications. 6625 Bamburgh Dr., San Diego, California 92117.

Kronos: A Journal of Interdisciplinary Synthesis. P. O. Box 343, Wynette, Pennsylvania 19096.

Newsletters:
Biblical Chronology. Institute for Christian Economics.

SCRIPTURE INDEX

OLD TESTAMENT

NEW TESTAMENT

INDEX

ABOUT THE AUTHOR

Gary North received his Ph.D. in history from the University of California, Riverside, in 1972. He is the author of approximately 30 books, and served as the editor of the *Journal of Christian Reconstruction* for its first eight years. He is the author of a multi-volume economic commentary on the Bible, *The Dominion Covenant*. His reviews and essays have appeared in about three dozen newspapers and periodicals, including the *Wall Street Journal*, *The Freeman*, *Modern Age*, *National Review*, *Westminster Theological Journal*, *Banner of Truth*, and *Journal of Political Economy*. He is the writer of two bi-monthly Christian newsletters, published by the Institute for Christian Economics: *Biblical Economics Today* and *Christian Reconstruction*. He is the publisher of several financial newsletters, including *Remnant Review*, *Low Profile*, *Clip Notes*, and *Investment Coin Review*, as well as the monthly bulletin, *Washington Report*. Three of his essays appear as appendixes in R. J. Rushdoony's *Institutes of Biblical Law* (1973). He lives with his wife and four children in east Texas.

ABOUT THE AUTHOR

WHAT IS THE ICE?

by Gary North, President, ICE

The Institute for Christian Economics is a non-profit, tax-exempt educational organization which is devoted to research and publishing in the field of Christian ethics. The perspective of those associated with the ICE is straightforwardly conservative and pro-free market. The ICE is dedicated to the proposition that biblical ethics requires full personal responsibility, and this responsible human action flourishes most productively within a framework of limited government, political decentralization, and minimum interference with the economy by the civil government.

For well over half a century, the loudest voices favoring Christian social action have been outspokenly pro-government intervention. Anyone needing proof of this statement needs to read Dr. Gregg Singer's comprehensive study, *The Unholy Alliance* (Arlington House Books, 1975), the definitive history of the National Council of Churches. An important policy statement from the National Council's General Board in 1967 called for *comprehensive economic planning*. The ICE was established in order to *challenge* statements like the following:

Accompanying this growing diversity in the structures of national life has been a growing recognition of the importance of competent planning within and among all resource sectors of the society: education, economic development, land use, social health services, the family system and congregational life. It is not generally recognized that an effective approach to problem solving requires a comprehensive planning process and coordination in the development of all these resource areas.

The *silence* from the conservative denominations in response to such policy proposals has been deafening. Not that conservative church members agree with such nonsense; they don't. But the conservative denominations and associations have remained silent because they have convinced themselves that *any* policy statement of any sort regarding social and economic life is *always* illegitimate. In short, there is no such thing as a correct, valid policy statement that a church or denomination can make. *The results of this opinion have been universally devastating.* The popular press assumes that the radicals who do speak out in the name of Christ are representative of the membership (or at least the press goes along with the illusion). The public is convinced that to speak out on social matters in the name of Christ is to be radical. *Christians are losing by default.*

The ICE is convinced that conservative Christians must devote resources to create alternative proposals. There is an old rule of political life which argues that "You can't beat something with nothing." We agree. It is not enough to adopt a whining negativism whenever someone or some group comes up with another nutty economic program. We need a comprehensive alternative.

Society or State

Society is broader than politics. The State is not a substitute for society. *Society encompasses all social institutions:* church, State, family, economy, kinship groups, voluntary clubs and associations, schools, and non-profit educational organizations (such as ICE). Can we say that there are no

standards of righteousness—justice—for these social institutions? Are they lawless? The Bible says no. We do not
live in a lawless universe. But this does not mean that the
State is the source of all law. On the contrary, God, not the
imitation god of the State, is the source.

Christianity is innately decentralist. *From the beginning,
orthodox Christians have denied the divinity of the State.* This is
why the Caesars of Rome had them persecuted and ex-
ecuted. They denied the operating presupposition of the
ancient world, namely, the legitimacy of a divine ruler or a
divine State.

It is true that modern liberalism has eroded Christian
orthodoxy. There are literally thousands of supposedly
evangelical pastors who have been compromised by the
liberalism of the universities and seminaries they attended.
The popularity, for example, of Prof. Ronald Sider's *Rich
Christians in an Age of Hunger,* co-published by InterVarsity
Press (evangelical Protestant) and the Paulist Press (liberal
Roman Catholic), is indicative of the crisis today. It has
sold like hotcakes, and it calls for mandatory wealth redis-
tribution by the State on a massive scale. Yet he is a professor at a Baptist seminary.

The ICE rejects the theology of the total State. This is
why we countered the book by Sider when we published David
Chilton's *Productive Christians in an Age of Guilt-Manipulators*
(3rd edition, 1985). Chilton's book shows that the Bible is
the foundation of our economic freedom, and that the call
for compulsory wealth transfers and higher taxes on the
rich is simply *baptized socialism.* Socialism is anti-Christian
to the core.

What we find is that laymen in evangelical churches
tend to be more conservative theologically and politically
than their pastors. But this conservatism is a kind of *instinc-*

tive conservatism. It is *not* self-consciously grounded in the Bible. So the laymen are unprepared to counter the sermons and Sunday School materials that bombard them week after week.

It is ICE's contention that *the only way to turn the tide in this nation is to capture the minds of the evangelical community,* which numbers in the tens of millions. We have to convince the liberal-leaning evangelicals of the biblical nature of the free market system. And we have to convince the conservative evangelicals of the same thing, in order to get them into the social and intellectual battles of our day.

In other words, *retreat is not biblical,* any more than socialism is.

By What Standard?

We have to ask ourselves this question: *"By what standard?"* By what standard do we evaluate the claims of the socialists and interventionists? By what standard do we evaluate the claims of the secular free market economists who reject socialism? By what standard are we to construct intellectual alternatives to the humanism of our day? And by what standard do we criticize the social institutions of our era?

If we say that the standard is "reason," we have a problem: Whose reason? If the economists cannot agree with each other, how do we decide who is correct? Why hasn't reason produced agreement after centuries of debate? We need an alternative.

It is the Bible. The ICE is dedicated to the defense of the Bible's reliability. But don't we face the same problem? Why don't Christians agree about what the Bible says concerning economics?

One of the main reasons why they do not agree is that the question of biblical economics has not been taken seriously. Christian scholars have ignored economic theory for generations. This is why the ICE devotes so much time, money, and effort to studying what the Bible teaches about economic affairs.

There will always be some disagreements, since men are not perfect, and their minds are imperfect. But when men agree about the basic issue of the starting point of the debate, they have a far better opportunity to discuss and learn than if they offer only "reason, rightly understood" as their standard.

Services

The ICE exists in order to serve Christians and other people who are vitally interested in finding moral solutions to the economic crisis of our day. The organization is a *support ministry* to other Christian ministries. It is non-sectarian, non-denominational, and dedicated to the proposition that a moral economy is a truly practical, productive economy.

The ICE produces several newsletters. These are aimed at intelligent laymen, church officers, and pastors. The reports are non-technical in nature. Included in our publication schedule are these monthly and bi-monthly publications:

Biblical Chronology (12 times a year)
Biblical Economics Today (6 times a year)
Christian Reconstruction (6 times a year)
Covenant Renewal (12 times a year)
Dispensationalism in Transition (12 times a year)

Biblical Chronology is devoted to studies in ancient history, with a view to helping lay foundations for Christian social theory and historiography. **Biblical Economics Today** is a four-page report that covers economic theory from a specifically Christian point of view. It also deals with questions of economic policy. **Christian Reconstruction** is more action-oriented, but it also covers various aspects of Christian social theory. **Covenant Renewal** explains the Biblical covenant and works out its implications for the three social institutions of culture: family, church and state. **Dispensationalism in Transition** has its emphasis on eschatology (doctrine of the endtimes). It challenges traditional Dispensationalism's "Code of Silence."

The purpose of the ICE is to relate biblical ethics to Christian activities in the field of economics. To cite the title of Francis Schaeffer's book, "How should we then live?" How should we apply biblical wisdom in the field of economics to our lives, our culture, our civil government, and our businesses and callings?

If God calls men to responsible decision-making, then He must have *standards of righteousness* that guide men in their decision-making. It is the work of the ICE to discover, illuminate, explain, and suggest applications of these guidelines in the field of economics. We publish the results of our findings in the newsletters.

The ICE sends out the newsletters free of charge. Anyone can sign up for six months to receive them. This gives the reader the opportunity of seeing "what we're up to." At the end of six months, he or she can renew for another six months.

Donors receive a one-year subscription. This reduces the extra trouble associated with sending out renewal notices, and it also means less trouble for the subscriber.

There are also donors who pledge to pay $10 a month. They are members of the ICE's *"Reconstruction Committee."* They help to provide a predictable stream of income which finances the day-to-day operations of the ICE. Then the donations from others can finance special projects, such as the publication of a new book.

The basic service that ICE offers is education. We are presenting ideas and approaches to Christian ethical behavior that few other organizations even suspect are major problem areas. *The Christian world has for too long acted as though we were not responsible citizens on earth,* as well as citizens of heaven. ("For our conversation [citizenship] is in heaven" [Philippians 3:20a].) *We must be godly stewards of all our assets,* which includes our lives, minds, and skills.

Because economics affects every sphere of life, the ICE's reports and surveys are relevant to all areas of life. Because *scarcity affects every area,* the whole world needs to be governed by biblical requirements for *honest stewardship* of the earth's resources. The various publications are wideranging, since the effects of the curse of the ground (Genesis 3:17-19) are wide-ranging.

What the ICE offers the readers and supporters is an introduction to a world of responsibility that few Christians have recognized. This limits our audience, since most people think they have too many responsibilities already. But if more people understood the Bible's solutions to economic problems, they would have more capital available to take greater responsibility — and prosper from it.

Finances

There ain't no such thing as a free lunch (TANSTAAFL). *Someone has to pay for those six-month renewable free subscriptions.* Existing donors are, in effect, supporting a kind of intellectual missionary organization. Except for the newsletters sent to ministers and teachers, we "clean" the mailing lists each year: less waste.

We cannot expect to raise money by emotional appeals. We have no photographs of starving children, no orphanages in Asia. We generate ideas. *There is always a very limited market for ideas, which is why some of them have to be subsidized by people who understand the power of ideas — a limited group, to be*

sure. John Maynard Keynes, the most influential econo-
mist of this century (which speaks poorly of this century),
spoke the truth in the final paragraph of his *General Theory of
Employment, Interest, and Money* (1936):

> . . . the ideas of economists and political philosophers, both
> when they are right and when they are wrong, are more powerful
> than is commonly understood. Indeed, the world is ruled by little
> else. Practical men, who believe themselves to be quite exempt
> from any intellectual influences, are usually the slaves of some de-
> funct economist. Madmen in authority, who hear voices in the
> air, are distilling their frenzy from some academic scribbler of a
> few years back. I am sure that the power of vested interests is
> vastly exaggerated compared with the gradual encroachment of
> ideas. Not, indeed, immediately, but after a certain interval; for
> in the field of economic and political philosophy there are not
> many who are influenced by new theories after they are twenty-
> five or thirty years of age, so that the ideas which civil servants
> and politicians and even agitators apply to current events are not
> likely to be the newest. But, soon or late, it is ideas, not vested in-
> terests, which are dangerous for good or evil.

Do you believe this? If so, then the program of long-term
education which the ICE has created should be of consider-
able interest to you. What we need are people with a *vested interest in ideas,* a *commitment to principle* rather than class position.

There will be few short-term, visible successes for the
ICE's program. There will be new and interesting books.
There will be a constant stream of newsletters. There will
be educational audio and video tapes. But the world is not
likely to beat a path to ICE's door, as long as today's
policies of high taxes and statism have not yet produced a
catastrophe. We are investing in the future, for the far side
of humanism's economic failure. *This is a long-term investment in intellectual capital.* Contact us at: **ICE, Box 8000,
Tyler, TX 75711.**